Tommy Douglas

Bill Waiser

Fitzhenry & Whiteside

Contents

THE CANADIANS ® *A Continuing Series*

Tommy Douglas

Copyright © 2006 by Bill Waiser

Fitzhenry & Whiteside, 195 Allstate Parkway, Markham, Ontario L3R 4T8

www.fitzhenry.ca   godwit@fitzhenry.ca

10 9 8 7 6 5 4 3 2 1

Library and Archives Canada Cataloguing in Publication
Waiser, W. A
Tommy Douglas / Bill Waiser.

(The Canadians) Includes index.
ISBN-13: 978-1-55041-944-3   ISBN-10: 1-55041-944-7

1. Douglas, T. C. (Thomas Clement), 1904-1986—Juvenile literature.
2. Saskatchewan—Politics and government—1944-1964—Juvenile literature.
3. Prime ministers—Saskatchewan—Biography—Juvenile literature.
4. Social reformers—Canada—Biography—Juvenile literature. I. Title.
II. Series: Canadians

FC3525.1.D68W33 2007   971.24'03092   C2006-905535-1

Fitzhenry & Whiteside acknowledges with thanks the Canada Council for the Arts, and the Ontario Arts Council for their support of our publishing program. We acknowledge the financial support of the Government of Canada through the Book Publishing Industry Development Program (BPIDP) for our publishing activities.

Canada Council   Conseil des Arts
for the Arts   du Canada

ONTARIO ARTS COUNCIL
CONSEIL DES ARTS DE L'ONTARIO

Cover illustration: John Mardon   Layout: Darrell McCalla
Printed and bound in Canada

The Most Unhappy Period of My Life

It was a charity case. The young, sickly boy, not even ten yet, was lying in a Winnipeg hospital ward, facing the horrible prospect of losing his right leg.

A few years earlier, Tommy Douglas had fallen and cut his knee on a stone while playing in his home village of Falkirk, Scotland. The wound failed to heal properly and osteomyelitis, a painful inflammation of the bone, had set in. A local doctor tried to get rid of the disease by operating on Tommy's leg on the family's kitchen table while his mother and grandmother assisted. But the painful scraping of his femur bone was not a success and the leg continued to bother him.

Emigrating to Canada with his family in 1911, Tommy spent months in and out of hospital, undergoing another three operations to try to fix his leg. And when he was not in hospital, he was hobbling around his Winnipeg neighbourhood on crutches or being pulled around in a small sleigh in winter. He would later call these years "the most unhappy period of my life."

Eventually, Tommy's doctors recommended amputating his leg and gave the family time to think about it. There seemed to be little choice, especially when Tommy's parents could not afford the services of a specialist. That's when fate intervened. A famous Winnipeg orthopaedic surgeon was going through the hospital ward one day and after examining Tommy's leg, proposed to take on the case as a teaching project for his students. Tommy's parents were anxious to do whatever they could to help their son and readily agreed, even though they were warned that the boy might lose movement in his knee. The operation, however, was a great success.

Tommy Douglas was extremely fortunate. He never forgot how his leg had been saved only because the Winnipeg doctor had taken him on as a charity case. The experience would have a profound influence on his life. He recalled in the 1950s, "I came to believe that health services ought not to have a price-tag on them, and that people should be able to get whatever health services they required irrespective of their individual capacity to pay." He was talking about what would become known as medicare.

Chapter 1
The Douglas Clan

Thomas Clement Douglas was born 20 October 1904 in Falkirk, Scotland, an industrial town between Edinburgh and Glasgow. Long before Falkirk became known for its iron foundries and steel mills, William Wallace of "Braveheart" fame fought a great battle here against King Edward of England.

Tommy's father was named Thomas Douglas and his father's father as well. Both men had worked as iron moulders. His mother, Anne Clement, was of northern stock and could count among her ancestors soldiers who had served with the Argyll and Sutherland Highlanders, fierce fighters in several wars at home and abroad.

Tommy grew up in a working-class setting, but was largely spared the poverty, filth, and misery that characterized much of industrial Scotland at the time. His father, as a skilled tradesman, earned a decent wage and was able to support a modest, though comfortable, home. He wanted a better life for his family, however, and often complained about the need for sweeping social reform and an end to the class distinctions that divided Scottish society. He was always talking about the issues of the day, usually at the dinner table or family gatherings, and his son was drawn into, in fact, expected, to take part in the friendly arguments.

Tommy's mother was a quieter force in the family, but no less influential. She kindled her son's interest in religion and his faith in the teachings of the Bible. She also encouraged a love of the arts, especially literature, and fired his imagination by reading to him from an early age. Tommy, at his mother's urging, would come to excel at public speaking, or oratory as it was called at the time. His favourite topic was the writings of Robbie Burns,

Scotland's national poet, and he learned to recite his work from memory, in many cases for inspiration. He also inherited his height from his mother. Whereas his father was tall and well built, Tommy was the exact opposite: short and spindly. He was often dismissed as puny, or worse, a runt. But what he lacked in size, he made up in temperament and could be bull-headed at times, especially when he believed he was right.

In 1910, Tommy's father, like thousands of other Scots in the early twentieth century, decided that Canada offered a more promising future and headed to Winnipeg with one of his brothers. Once he landed a job with the Vulcan Iron Works, he sent for his wife, Anne, Tommy, and daughter Nan; a second daughter, Isobel, would soon be born in Canada. Tommy's family arrived in the capital of Manitoba aboard a colonist train in April 1911 and literally stepped off into a strange new world.

Winnipeg was the first city of the prairies, the Gateway to the West, the Chicago of Canada. Boasting a population of 136,000 at the time — a three-fold increase since the beginning of the century — it owed its rise to the railways, the grain business, the wholesale trade, the manufacturing industries, the financial offices, and of course, the hundreds of thousands of settlers they served throughout the region. All of these activities required a large labour force — hence, the booming population. The city's

Winnipeg's Main Street was a bustling part of the city when Tommy Douglas and his family arrived in 1911.

Tommy Douglas

future seemed to be limitless if the hustle and bustle on the streets were any indication.

Winnipeg was also at the forefront of the social reform movement. The city's rapid growth had led to overcrowded, impoverished slum neighbourhoods, where the child mortality rate rivalled that of the less developed world. An equally serious problem was drinking. Because the first wave of immigrants during the set- tlement boom were over- whelmingly young single men, Winnipeg boasted over 200 saloons, pool halls, liquor retailers, and broth- els in its downtown core. Prohibitionists readily believed that booze was at the root of most of society's problems — from crime to poverty to family neglect —

Portage Avenue in Winnipeg, around 1912

and argued that its elimination would work miracles. The "ban- ish the bar" movement, however, made little headway, and women began to demand the right to vote to bring about the reform. Among them was Nellie McClung, the outspoken female suffrage leader, who ridiculed the Manitoba premier in her famous mock Parliament at Winnipeg's Walker Theatre.

But what made the bustling city unique, especially for a young boy fresh from Scotland, was that Tommy found himself thrown in a kind of cultural crucible. His new friends in his Winnipeg inner-city neighbourhood were so-called foreigners from continental Europe with strange customs, strange languages, even strange ways of dressing. Because they were widely regarded as a threat to the British character of Canadian society, these immigrants faced discrimination, if not outright contempt. Tommy quickly learned, however, that immigrant families, what- ever their ethnic origin, were just trying to get ahead like every- one else and that racism stood in their way. "They were wrestling

Winnipeg's North End, home to thousands of recent immigrants, was notorious for its poverty.

with the same problems we were," he later observed. "You found that you were basically the same."

Shortly after the Douglas family arrived in Winnipeg, the Canadian economy slid into a recession that lasted until after the outbreak of the Great War in 1914. The prairies were particularly hard hit, as falling grain prices hurt other sectors of the region's economy. These were difficult years for Tommy's family, made worse by his bout with osteomyelitis, and they survived as best they could on his father's reduced hours. Unskilled immigrants were not so lucky and soon swelled the growing ranks of the unemployed.

The "one fortunate bright spot," to use Tommy's words, was All People's Mission, only a few blocks from his Winnipeg home. Headed by J.S. Woodsworth, a Methodist minister who wanted "new Canadians" assimilated, the mission doubled as a community centre for local immigrant boys and girls. Here, they could play sports and other games or simply borrow a book from its library in addition to attending one of Woodsworth's sermons. Tommy, when not in the hospital, was a regular visitor and always appreciated what the mission meant to kids from poor homes. Little did he realize, though, that he would cross paths with Woodsworth many more times.

Canada went to war at Great Britain's side in 1914. Tommy's dad, a veteran of the Boer War in South Africa, refused to watch from the sidelines. He took his family back to Scotland, where he enlisted in a medical unit. Tommy, his mom, and two sisters waited out the war in Glasgow, living in a small apartment with his maternal grandparents.

It was another stressful period in Tommy's life, what with his father gone and the many sacrifices demanded by the war. He also disliked the strict discipline in the public school he attended. But he found happiness in the fact that his leg had mended and he could play soccer and other games. He also became quite adept at defending himself with his fists and claimed to have had a fight almost every school day.

In September 1918, Tommy did not return to high school but took an office job in a local cork factory to help his family. He was not even fourteen. The owner of the business wanted to train him as a cork buyer who would travel to Spain and Portugal several times a year. Tommy, meanwhile, had dreams of going to sea as a sailor one day. But then the war ended in November and his dad, who had survived a gas attack, came home on leave.

J.S. Woodsworth in Ottawa, 1923

Tommy's father had originally planned to remain in Scotland after his family's return from Canada. He was more than ever disillusioned, however, by the old class distinctions. He was worried that the lack of opportunity would force his son to follow him into the foundry, as he had followed his own dad. He consequently decided to send his family back to Winnipeg; he would take his discharge there. New Year's Day in 1919 found Tommy's family at sea. They were bound for Canada to start over again.

Chapter 2
Winnipeg

Tommy Douglas was excited to be returning to Canada. Certainly the years in Winnipeg before the war had not been easy for his family, but it had more to offer someone in their early teens than Falkirk or Glasgow. He had also reached a new stage in his life. His mother and two sisters were now counting on him until his father was demobilized and able to join them. In a way, he was no longer a boy, but had taken on the responsibilities of a man. And he accepted them without complaint.

Tommy's first job in Winnipeg, after buying a bicycle, was as an errand boy for a drugstore. He stayed at that for a few weeks

Winnipeg's City Hall and Market Square

until he found other messenger jobs that paid more money. But he soon craved something more permanent and signed on as an apprentice with the *Grain Trade News*. It would take five years to become a journeyman printer. Tommy started at the bottom as a printer's devil, stripping and melting the lead type and breaking up and cleaning the forms that held the type together. Within a few months, he was setting type.

Tommy joined the Typographical Union in 1919, a pivotal point in Canadian labour history. The Great War had soured the mood and outlook of Winnipeg workers. They were upset that their wages had not kept pace with the spiralling wartime prices for food, clothing, fuel, and rent. Thanks to the sharp rise in the cost of living, most found themselves worse off at the end of the war than they had been in 1914. It was a feeling shared by many veterans upon their return to Canada, including Tommy's father, who were disillusioned by how little had been changed despite their bloody sacrifice. The business community, by contrast, not only seemed to have fared much better, but portrayed unions as a threat to its profits and did everything it could to undermine their influence.

Workers tried to make up for their losses during the war years by negotiating better settlements with their employers. But when these efforts were rebuffed, delegates at a western labour conference in Calgary in the spring of 1919 chose a more radical course of action. They resoundingly endorsed the proposal to bring both skilled and unskilled workers together in larger unions along industrial lines (what was known as the One Big Union movement) and to employ radical tactics, such as the

general strike, to force employers to accede to their demands. Only a few weeks later, by sheer coincidence, the building and metal trades in Winnipeg went on strike over the issues of collective bargaining and higher wages.

The Winnipeg walkout soon escalated into a general strike, when tens of thousands left their jobs in sympathy on May 15 and effectively paralyzed western Canada's

largest city for more than a month. Even milk delivery was temporarily suspended. Winnipeg became a divided city as employers and more affluent citizens lined up against the striking workers. Tommy sided with the strikers and spent any spare time he had wandering the crowded streets, when he was not attending outdoor meetings. One of the most impassioned speakers was his former

The Winnipeg General Strike in 1919 paralyzed western Canada's largest city for more than a month.

minister, J.S. Woodsworth, who had left the Methodist Church in 1918 in protest against its support of the war effort. Woodsworth, a strong supporter of the trade union movement, talked about how labour had legitimate grievances and had every right to demand a decent wage.

The federal government saw things differently, much differently. In the wake of the 1917 Russian Revolution, Ottawa dreaded the export of communism to the shores of Canada. And by using the weapon of a general strike, the workers in Winnipeg gave substance to public fears of an international Bolshevik conspiracy. The fact that the strike leaders were from British backgrounds was deliberately ignored in favour of highlighting the large number of foreigners with unpronounceable last names in the Winnipeg labour force. Were they not carrying the seeds of sedition? Some even argued that the city was a testing ground for the One Big Union idea. It is little wonder, then, that the federal government, with the blessing of the Winnipeg business community, used the Royal Northwest Mounted Police to crush the strike.

Tommy personally witnessed the police action that day. On 23 June 1919, Bloody Saturday as it became known, the young printer's apprentice and a few friends climbed atop a building to watch a showdown between the strikers and armed mounties on horseback. When demonstrators taking part in a protest parade failed to disperse when ordered, the police made three charges to clear the street, firing their guns into the crowd. Two men were killed and many more wounded. One of the victims fell not far from Tommy's viewing place. The strike ended days later.

Tommy Douglas watched from a rooftop as the mounted police charged through the crowd on Winnipeg's Main Street.

Tommy, only fourteen at the time, was deeply troubled by the turn of events. "Certainly, as the years went by," he later recounted, "the Winnipeg General Strike left a very lasting impression on me ... Whenever the powers that be can't get what they want, they're always prepared to resort to violence ... to break the back of organized opposition." That included arresting Woodsworth, who was charged with publishing editorials in a strikers' newspaper that criticized the authorities.

Winnipeg workers grudgingly returned to their jobs after the strike with nothing to show for their walkout. Tommy continued to work in the print shop, while attending school a few nights each week to improve his skills. By sixteen, he was running a linotype machine (the machine that produced the lead print type) and getting journeyman's wages, even though he had not served his full five-year apprenticeship. He was reportedly the youngest linotype operator in Canada. Interestingly, the various printing jobs piqued his interest in a number of subjects, and he tried to do further reading.

Tommy also somehow managed a busy social life. Through his church, he served as a Cub master and assistant Scout leader in his Elmwood neighbourhood. He would often take his boys by bicycle on weekend camping trips just east of the city. He also took speaking lessons and did small parts in local productions, sometimes at the Walker Theatre, and entertained at concerts and special dinners. His Scottish accent made him a popular choice for Robbie Burns celebrations. In time, he perfected the art of the monologue and sometimes performed before hundreds of people. This experience would serve him well.

Tommy's great passion at this time, though, was boxing. He started training at a local gym and had his first bout in the light-weight class when he was fifteen. Despite his size — he was only 61 kilograms — he was a scrappy competitor, and claimed the Manitoba lightweight championship in 1922. It came at the cost of a broken nose, two lost teeth, and a sprained thumb. Tommy's parents hated to see their son hurt and refused to come to any of his fights. But he climbed back into the ring the following year in a rematch with the former champion and easily defended his title. What was especially amazing about his victories was that he was known for his speedy footwork. This was the same boy who had nearly lost his leg to osteomyelitis a decade earlier.

Chapter 3
The Ministry

Tommy Douglas made a good living in the Winnipeg printing business. In fact, he was bringing home more money than his dad. But many of the people who came to know him suggested that he should try his hand at something that would make greater use of his talents, especially his speaking skills. There was also the matter of his education. He had quit school at fourteen and might never secure his diploma if he continued in the printing trade.

In 1922, Tommy decided to enter the ministry. Although his parents had never interfered in his choice of careers, his mother, Anne, was extremely pleased. "She told me," Tommy remembered, "that this was what she had always hoped I would do." He felt much the same way. "The general feeling," he admitted, "was that if I had any useful contribution to make at all it was probably in the Christian church."

In retrospect, becoming a minister was a logical next step for the eighteen-year-old. Tommy had joined the Baptist Church when he first came to Canada, and since then, had always been involved in church activities. In particular, he greatly enjoyed the fellowship of the young people's meetings and wanted the opportunity to work with young boys and try to make a difference in their lives. The church seemed to be the answer. Or at least, it was calling him. His minister would sometimes ask him to take over the Sunday evening service. He found that he liked preaching, liked church work in general.

To get to college, Tommy first had to find the money and he spent a year saving whatever did not go towards supporting the family household; he could not count on his parent's financial support and did not want to. He also borrowed books from his

friends and spent time reading and studying in preparation for
his classes. Tommy had been out of school for four years and
wanted to be ready when he finally resumed his education.

More important, though, was finding another source of
income, since he would be giving up his job in the printing business. Here, Tommy was helped by the Manitoba Superintendent
of Missions who found him work as a supply preacher in small
country churches outside Winnipeg. At one of his first postings,
the congregation wondered who the kid was taking the service.
But they happily invited the preacher with the boyish looks back
the following Sunday.

Tommy entered Brandon College in September 1924, one
month shy of his twentieth birthday. He would be there for six
years, completing his high school requirements and then his the-
ology training. These were difficult days for organized religion in
Canada. In 1925, members of the Methodist and Congregational
churches, along with some Presbyterian congregations, came
together to form the United Church of Canada. The new church
placed less emphasis on personal salvation and the after-life in
favour of applying the teachings of Christ to everyday social
problems — what was known as the "social gospel." The goal
was to bring about the "Kingdom of God on earth." Some
Protestant denominations, however, continued to support a more
traditional or literal interpretation of the Bible and heaped scorn
on the social gospel enthusiasts.

These tensions were played out within the walls of Brandon
College, as faculty and students argued over the meaning of the
Scriptures. One of the most controversial instructors, a professor
of the New Testament, was a modernist who openly challenged
the fundamentalists and their deep-seated convictions. He gave
the Gospel, in Tommy's words, "a new meaning" by speaking "of
the spirit in men's hearts ... of righteousness and justice." Some
found this thinking too radical, others admired it and the conviction with which it was voiced. Tommy was one of those he won
over. "It liberalized my views," he confessed.

Tommy had the opportunity to put these influences into practice as he continued to preach on weekends and throughout the

summers to earn some money. On his way to start college in Brandon, he had been asked to conduct the last service in a church in Austin, Manitoba, that was closing because of divisions within the congregation. At the end of his sermon, he was invited to be the regular preacher. It was later decided that Tommy would come to Austin every other weekend. He served there for two years before being approached to take over the Presbyterian Church in Carberry even though he was a Baptist. That lasted for another two years before he was reclaimed by the Baptists to handle the services in Shoal Lake near Dauphin.

Tommy Douglas served as a student minister in Carberry, Manitoba, in the mid-1920s.

Tommy's preaching honed his public speaking skills. To earn extra cash, he also entertained clubs and other groups in the Brandon area, usually telling humorous stories from his growing personal repertoire. He was much like today's stand-up comic, but instead of a series of jokes, he told stories with amusing insights. Often he exchanged barbs with his audience and believed that the best jokes were those that got the better of him. He was never afraid to laugh at himself — if it was deserved.

Tommy was also heavily involved in extracurricular activities at the college. He served on the executive of the student body, culminating in his position as "senior stick," or chairman, in his final year. His favourite club was the debating society and he loved the thrust and parry of the competition. Tommy never regretted the time that he devoted to these college activities at the expense of his academic work. "Looking back on it," he once mused, they were "maybe more important ... I learned a great deal about working with people and helping organize activities." These abilities would be called upon in the future.

Tommy was scheduled to graduate in the spring of 1930. The big question was where he was going to be posted. Over the past winter, he and Stanley Knowles, another Brandon student and future parliamentarian, had preached alternate Sundays at Calvary Baptist Church in Weyburn, Saskatchewan, a city of about 5,000 on a CPR branch line running southeast from Regina. The congregation wanted to size up both preachers before making a choice. In the end, the nod went to Tommy, largely because of his interest in young people, and he was ordained in the church in June 1930. He would turn twenty-six in four months.

Douglas became the minister at Calvary Baptist Church in Weyburn, Saskatchewan, in 1930.

The year 1930 was an eventful one in Tommy's life. He graduated, was ordained, and secured his own church. But that was not all that happened. While preaching in Carberry, he met Irma Dempsey, whom he got to know through his community work. In fact, Irma, a Methodist, was so interested in the young new preacher in town that she started to attend Tommy's services at the Presbyterian Church in Carberry. She then moved to Brandon to study music as part of her training as a teacher. And that's where the pair was married on 30 June 1930.

Tommy jokingly claimed that Irma's father, a horse dealer, consented to the union because his future son-in-law knew about horses from his days in Scotland. Tommy's brother-in-law, also a minister, performed the service, while Stanley Knowles stood up as his best man. The newlyweds spent their honeymoon in Winnipeg, visiting Tommy's parents, before starting their new life together in Weyburn. It could be said that Calvary Baptist got not one, but two, workers.

Chapter 4

The Dirty Thirties

T ommy Douglas could not have started his new posting at a worse time. In the mid-1920s, while Great Britain and the rest of Europe were recovering from the destruction of the Great War, North America roared to unprecedented heights of growth and prosperity. But by the end of the decade, the international demand for goods — and the prices for them — collapsed because of overproduction. The famous stock market crash of 1929 was a direct consequence of this instability in the world economy. And the situation went from bad to worse when countries tried to protect their domestic economies by erecting high trade barriers that further restricted the flow of goods. The result was the Great Depression.

Saskatchewan was one of the first casualties of the economic crisis. Much of the province's prosperity in the 1920s had been

Harvest time, 1928

fuelled by the sale of wheat on the export market. Now, on the eve of the new decade, agriculture was hit with a double whammy. Not only did international demand for wheat evaporate, but the price went into a free fall. The 1932 harvest, for example, sold for only thirty-five cents a bushel, the lowest price for wheat in centuries.

The repercussions were nothing short of catastrophic, all the more so for a province and a people whose livelihood rested almost exclusively on wheat. Many farmers simply could not stay afloat, and when they went down, they took with them other sectors of the provincial economy, like the vortex created by a sinking ship. Not even urban centres were spared. Because towns and cities, such as Weyburn, acted primarily as agricultural service centres, businesses floundered, unemployment soared, and tax arrears mounted as the price of wheat went into a tailspin. By the end of the 1930s, Saskatchewan was the most indebted province in the country.

The other nightmare was the prolonged drought, which placed a stranglehold on the southern prairies and would not let go for the better part of the decade. Severe droughts had always been a persistent feature of the region, occurring on average every twenty years or so. The 1930s, however, were notorious for the number of consecutive dry years. On 5 July 1937, both Midale and Yellowgrass, not far from Weyburn, reached 45 degrees Celsius, the hottest temperature ever recorded in Canada. "We went years without any rain and without any crop," Douglas remembered. "There was no water for livestock, to keep chickens alive, for gardening."

The hot, drying winds scooped up loose topsoil and whipped it into towering dust storms that made outside activity in places like Weyburn nearly impossible. Darkness at noon was not uncommon, while churning soil piled up in deep drifts along buildings, fence lines, or ridges — anything that stood in the way of the swirling dust. During the storms, mothers were known to put lamps by windows so that children could find their way home from school. They also faced a frustrating battle trying to keep the dust out of their homes, setting wet rags on window sills and hanging wet sheets over doorways. But it still managed to seep through.

The weather spawned all kinds of exaggerated stories. One of the most popular legends was that children reached school age before knowing what rain was or came running home in fright when they felt a drop of rain for the first time. Another was that parents decided whether to send their children outside by throwing a gopher up in the air; if the animal dug a burrow, then there was too much dust swirling around. Then there was the story of the young baseball player who lost his direction while rounding the bases during a dust storm and was later found several miles out on the prairie.

Since Canada had experienced severe recessions before, most expected the worst of the downturn to be over in a year, maybe two, and that traditional practices, like cutting expenditures and laying off employees, would tide the country over until the recovery kicked in. No one at the time realized that the downswing would last until 1933 when the unemployment rate hit a lofty thirty percent, which translated into 1.5 million Canadians out of work. Some regions of the country like Saskatchewan would not see a rebound until the latter part of the decade.

There was also no unemployment insurance in Canada at the time. It was widely believed before the Depression that, if an individual was provided with any kind of income support, then not only would the individual stop looking for a job, but others would be discouraged from seeking work as well. The truly destitute, however, did not go without any help. Under the Canadian constitution, the provision of relief, as it was called, was a local responsibility.

What this meant was that municipal relief boards and private church-run charities were quickly overwhelmed by the needs of the unemployed, even though assistance was deliberately kept to the minimum necessary to keep someone alive. To make matters worse, accepting relief carried with it the burden of personal failure and disgrace. Indeed, many Canadians were too ashamed to ask for help. Any relief assistance, moreover, was largely directed at men, because they were seen by society as breadwinners. The care of the female unemployed was understood to be a family matter, not the role of the state.

Tommy Douglas

This was the situation that Douglas stepped into when he assumed his duties as a minister in Weyburn. He knew from past church work that a minister's life was more than delivering sermons and that he would be expected to be a presence in the community, ready to counsel young people, visit the sick and elderly, or simply listen to someone's troubles. But nothing had prepared him for the steady traffic to the church's doors — transients looking for their next meal or local townspeople and district farmers wanting some help. While the outlying farm community battled the twin forces of drought and depression, unemployment in Weyburn grew by leaps and bounds.

Two of the biggest needs were food and clothing. Through an arrangement with other Protestant churches, carloads of apples and vegetables were shipped from British Columbia. Douglas spent days emptying the boxcars with a scoop shovel, filling up sacks, baskets, and anything else that people brought with them. He also spearheaded clothing drives, collecting second-hand items or old stock from storekeepers. One day, Douglas stopped a mother of a large family as she was leaving Sunday service. She never asked for help and never would. When Douglas asked how her children were fixed for clothing, she replied, holding back tears, "Well, they haven't got any winter underwear, so I've been trying to make some out of flour sacks." She was given bedding and clothes before she left for home.

Some families abandoned their farms in the drought area and headed north to start over.

The Dirty Thirties

Douglas was instrumental in organizing the Weyburn unemployed in the fall of 1931. He turned an old, abandoned house into an employment agency. Anyone who had work of any kind, from snow shovelling to pulling weeds to simple home repairs, could contact the office and a man would be sent for a nominal fee. It was not much, but at least the jobless could hold their heads up. Some in the community, though, believed that Douglas was overstepping the bounds of his work, especially when he locked horns with provincial relief officers over how the government was handling the crisis. But he could not keep quiet when needy families lacked coal for heating and milk for their children.

Douglas was also troubled by what poverty was doing to families. "I buried a young man at Griffin, and another one at Pangman," he sadly recounted years later, "both young men in their thirties, who died because there was no doctor readily available, and they hadn't the money to get proper care. They were buried in coffins made by local people out of ordinary wood." He equally regretted how young

Single, homeless, unemployed men line up for food.

people were being forced to give up their dreams after completing high school, if they had not already quit school to help their families. For Douglas, they were being cheated of the opportunity to do something with their lives. Something had to change.

Chapter 5
Such a Mess

Tommy Douglas believed that the church had a moral duty to grapple with the social and economic problems of the 1930s in order to bring about a better world. "We had to concern ourselves," he observed, "with the problems people had here and now ... as Christians we can't be indifferent to how people live and what their daily problems are." That's why he devoted so much time and energy to the poor of Weyburn.

This faith in what the church could achieve would be sorely tested during the Depression. During the summer of 1931, Douglas travelled to Chicago as part of his studies for a post-graduate degree. He spent three weeks interviewing some of the tens of thousands of homeless transients in the large, squalid hobo jungle on the outskirts of the city. Many were fresh-faced teens feeling hopeless about their fate as society's outcasts. It was a sobering experience. He later stated, "Those case histories ... really shook me ... The only difference is that I had a job, and they didn't."

A hobo jungle

When Douglas returned home, he started to "read and think and inquire why we were in such a mess." He had lots of questions, but there were no ready answers. "I'd never sat down and honestly asked myself what was wrong with the economic system," he admitted. "I think most people in the church were exactly the same. We'd taken it for granted. We'd accepted it. But here we were facing poverty, misery, want, lack of medical care, and lack of opportunity."

He grudgingly realized that his congregation at Weyburn's Calvary Baptist Church was doing everything humanly possible to alleviate the suffering caused by the Great Depression, but making little headway. Maybe some form of socialism, whereby the means of production was collectively shared for the benefit of all, was the way to bring about the "Kingdom of God on earth."

It was while trying to make sense of the situation that he saw the heavy hand of government and the police at work again, this time in southeastern Saskatchewan. In early September 1931, the miners in the nearby Estevan-Bienfait coalfields overwhelmingly voted to join the communist-led Mine Worker's Union of Canada in an effort to improve their working conditions. But when the mine owners refused to recognize the new union, 600 workers put down their tools and stayed off the job in peaceful protest until the union question was resolved.

Later that month, when the mine owners and operators started using scab (replacement) labour, the union organizers decided

Armed mounted policemen confronted striking miners and their families in Estevan in September 1931.

Tommy Douglas

to hold a sympathy parade in Estevan on September 29, hence-forth known locally as Black Tuesday. As the motorcade reached the town, the striking miners, along with their wives and families, were confronted with an armed cordon of mounted police block-ing the main street. A vicious battle ensued. When the fighting was over, three miners were dead, while several others, including local citizens, were wounded. Douglas, who had delivered food hampers to the miners during their strike, responded with a stinging sermon in which he asked how "Jesus the Revolutionary" would have viewed the current crisis.

What happened in Estevan was eerily reminiscent of Winnipeg, and gave Douglas's Baptist faith a sharp reformist edge. He responded by redoubling his efforts to reach out to local workers by helping them form the Weyburn Independent Labour Association. He was also regularly invited to address groups of farmers in the district. The Depression had pushed a growing number of angry farmers in the direction of more radi-cal reform. Losing money on every bushel of wheat they tried to harvest and facing the loss of the family farm to creditors, they began to see initiatives such as government planning as the answer. When some farm leaders pitched the idea of a larger

The Great Depression sparked calls to reform the capitalist system.

Such a Mess

political organization that would bring various like-minded organizations under the same umbrella, Douglas volunteered to write to his old friend J.S. Woodsworth for advice.

Woodsworth had been serving in the House of Commons since 1921 as the Labour Member of Parliament for Winnipeg North Centre. Known as the "conscience of Canada," he had worked tirelessly to bring about a system of public ownership and socialized planning through pragmatic, democratic means — as opposed to Marxist revolutionary socialism. His efforts paid only a few dividends, such as the adoption of old-age pensions in 1927.

But the Depression gave his message new meaning, and he began to collaborate with labour, socialist, and other groups to form a new federal party.

Woodsworth, fondly remembering the young Tommy, suggested to Douglas that he contact M.J. Coldwell, a long-time Regina school principal and alderman who by 1931 headed the new province-wide Independent Labour Party (ILP). Coldwell advocated a moderate reform socialism to resolve the grievances of the province's working-class population. He once said that "socialism meant simply putting into practice the principles of Christian brotherhood." Like many others wrestling with the problems of the Depression, he also believed that it was time to bring farmer and labour groups together to create a new political force in Saskatchewan.

Tommy Douglas and his good friend M.J. Coldwell later in life

On a Saturday afternoon in the late spring of 1932, Coldwell called on Douglas at the Calvary Baptist Church; he found the preacher in the library preparing the next day's sermon. It was the beginning of a long and warm friendship. The two chatted about the situation and decided that the first step was to bring the Weyburn Independent Labour Association into the

Independent Labour Party. A somewhat reluctant Douglas agreed to serve as president. Later that July in Saskatoon, delegates from the ILP and the United Farmers of Canada (Saskatchewan Section) voted to fight the next provincial election on a socialist platform as the Farmer-Labour Party (FLP).

Douglas could not attend the founding meeting of the Farmer-Labour Party. Nor was he there in Calgary in August 1932 when several farmer and labour groups from across the country agreed to form a new national party, the Co-operative Commonwealth Federation (CCF). But he was present at the first CCF convention in Regina in July 1933, at which J.S. Woodsworth was selected leader and the party's official platform, known as the Regina Manifesto, was vigorously debated and adopted. The last sentence of the manifesto had the ring of revolution: "No CCF Government will rest content until it has eradicated capitalism and put into operation the full program of socialized planning which will lead to the establishment in Canada of the Co-operative Commonwealth."

Douglas was no revolutionary. Nor were Coldwell and Woodsworth for that matter. But they were outraged by the

The national CCF met in Regina in 1933 to endorse a formal party platform, known as the Regina Manifesto.

Such a Mess

poverty, deprivation, and hopelessness of the 1930s and turned to Christian socialism as the answer. In other words, they combined the practical teachings of the Bible with a gradual, social democratic reform.

George Williams, one of the founders of the FLP, tried to explain the new party's position in a 1932 pamphlet, *What is Socialism?*: "Socialism does not mean ... that if you have two shirts you must give one to your friend ... It does mean that no one will be obliged to go without a shirt." This political philosophy certainly dovetailed with Douglas's way of looking at the world. Whether it would draw him into politics was another matter.

Chapter 6
The Candidate

Tommy Douglas was ready to step back once the Farmer-Labour Party had been formed. He believed that the disaffected groups had at last found a political vehicle for their grievances and that he could now "drop out and get on with my work." In fact, it did not occur to him at the time that he would one day run for office, let alone pursue a political career. But when a provincial election was called for July 1934, Douglas was forced to run for the new party when no one else was willing to put his name forward.

The first-time candidate faced a political battlefield in flux. The government, led by Conservative J.T.M. Anderson, had become identified with the Depression during its five years in office. It was widely assumed that the party was going down to defeat — the question was: How badly? The Opposition Liberals under former Saskatchewan premier Jimmy Gardiner portrayed themselves as the practical, reform alternative to the Anderson government. They also rightly realized that the Farmer-Labour Party represented the real roadblock to returning to power and told the electorate that the choice was between Liberalism and socialism.

A political meeting in Regina in the early 1930s

The Liberal campaign strategy was ironically given a boost by the FLP's controversial "use lease" policy, which effectively

proposed that the government control all land and lease it to farmers. This smacked of the land policy in Soviet Russia in the 1930s and was often held up to substantiate the claim that the FLP was a revolutionary group. The FLP insisted that it was not necessarily against private ownership; rather, it was against the evils of monopoly capitalism, which allowed mortgage companies to seize land from struggling farmers. But the "use lease" policy made people nervous, and the new party had to work hard to educate the public about its particular brand of socialism and how it stood for peaceful, constitutional change.

In the Weyburn riding, Douglas ran what he called an educational campaign. He held meetings in homes and rural schools where he talked about the prob-

Tommy Douglas, the political candidate

lems of the capitalist system. "I had charts and so on," he recounted, "and I'm sure half the people didn't know what I was talking about." Douglas also found himself answering all kinds of questions, such as "if it was true we were going to take away the people's farms." Despite such nagging concerns about the party's agenda, he was confident of victory.

Saskatchewan voters delivered a landslide in the 1934 election — but not for the FLP. In one of the most lopsided victories in the province's electoral history, the Liberals won fifty of the fifty-five seats in the Legislature. The Conservatives were denied a single seat. What the overwhelming Liberal victory tended to obscure, though, was the FLP's emergence as the official Opposition, thanks to the election of five candidates, thereafter known as "the quints." Douglas was not among them. He had come third in his riding.

Tommy Douglas

Many predicted a short life for Saskatchewan's new opposition party. As T.C. Davis, the new Liberal attorney general, quipped, "it came with the Depression and the grasshoppers and it would disappear with the Depression and the grasshoppers." But Saskatchewan politics had undergone a fundamental revolution with the election of FLP candidates and would never be the same again.

Douglas, however, did not see himself taking part in the struggles ahead. He had run against his own better judgment — "done my duty," to use his words — and wanted to get back to church work or study for his doctorate and look for a university position. Besides, there were new demands at home: the birth of a daughter, Shirley.

Douglas's desire to stay out of politics was regretted by his supporters, who were urging him to contest the next federal election as a Co-operative Commonwealth Federation candidate. But he remained adamant that he was not going to run. Then, just before the nomination meeting, he was visited by the superintendent of the Baptist Church in western Canada. The church official had interviewed members of Douglas's congregation and learned that most supported his recent venture into politics. At the same time, he admonished Douglas, "This is to be the last. You're not to run again." When the preacher replied that people wanted him to try for the federal seat, he was bluntly told, "Leave it ... and if you don't ... you'll never get another church in Canada." Douglas shot back, "You've just given the CCF a candidate."

This decision was reinforced a few days later when Stanley Knowles, Tommy's friend from his Brandon school days, wrote to ask whether Douglas was going to run in the upcoming general election. Knowles added that many of his friends in the church were counting on him being a candidate. Douglas talked the matter over with Irma, and together they agreed he should seek the nomination — even if it meant being struck off the rolls of the Baptist Church.

The federal election campaign in October 1935 featured the most parties and the most candidates ever to run in a Canadian election. All had their own solutions about how to deal with the

Depression. Like the Anderson government in Saskatchewan, the ruling Conservatives under R.B. Bennett had become synonymous with hard times. The prime minister was also disliked in the province for his rough handling of the On-to-Ottawa Trek when he ordered the RCMP to arrest the Trek leaders at a peaceful rally in downtown Regina on Dominion Day in 1935. The police raid provoked a riot that left two dead, hundreds injured, and tens of thousands of dollars of damage to the city. Douglas was there the night of the riot.

The battle for Weyburn was hotly contested. The incumbent Liberal candidate made wild claims about the CCF and how it would destroy the country. Douglas countered by attending Liberal meetings and challenging questionable statements made against him and the party. He also widely publicized his opponent's statement in the House of Commons that Canadians had to accept a lower standard of living. Eventually, the pair went head-to-head in the Weyburn arena in a debate attended by several thousand people. The venue was a perfect setting for someone with Douglas's oratorical skills and his performance that night turned the campaign in his favour.

But would he remain the CCF candidate? Douglas had been quietly co-operating with the new Social Credit Party, which had moved into Saskatchewan fresh from its overwhelming victory in the 1935 Alberta election. It appears that he was trying to prevent the protest vote from being split between the two parties. The CCF, however, was officially against any collaboration with Social Credit and demanded an explanation less than one week before the election. A pugnacious Douglas refused to admit to any wrongdoing and was allowed to continue in the race when Coldwell intervened on his behalf.

On election day, the Liberals under Mackenzie King stormed back into office with the largest number of seats (173) in any Parliament up to that time. Their election policy was to have no policy, or as the Liberal campaign slogan aptly put it: "It's King or Chaos." The CCF, running on the Regina Manifesto, won only seven seats nationally, including Douglas and Coldwell in Saskatchewan.

In June 1935, over 1,000 single, homeless, unemployed men clamoured aboard boxcars in Vancouver to take their complaints about the government's relief policy directly to the prime minister. The On-to-Ottawa Trek gained momentum as it headed eastward but was stopped in Regina by the RCMP. A riot broke out in downtown Regina when the police tried to break up a peaceful rally of Trekkers and citizens on Dominion Day.

Douglas had to wait until the next morning to find out whether he had been elected because of the returns arriving late from rural areas along the Canada-U.S. border. He carried the riding by just over 300 votes. The church superintendent, meanwhile, never followed through on his threat and Douglas remained a Baptist minister in good standing. But his formal days as a preacher were over. His payment from Calvary Baptist at the end of December 1935 would be his last. The church has since been moved to a new Weyburn location and serves today as the T.C. Douglas Calvary Centre for the Performing Arts.

Chapter 7

Never Let Them Down

Fresh from his election victory, Tommy and Irma Douglas along with baby Shirley travelled to Winnipeg for the 1935 Christmas holidays. Douglas's parents were quite proud, especially his dad who had quietly hoped that his son would go into politics. The elder Tom, who was normally spare in his praise, even offered some advice. "Now remember, laddie," he told his son, "the working people have put a lot of trust in you, you must never let them down." It would be the last time that Douglas would see his father. He died of peritonitis early in the new year. Douglas attended the funeral on his way to Ottawa and took comfort in the fact that his dad had lived to see him elected to the House of Commons.

Douglas, at thirty-one, had never visited the Parliament Buildings, never been to Ottawa before. Now he was taking his place on the back benches. The election results had been a great disappointment to the party, and its small numbers in the House meant that each and every CCF member would have to work especially hard to get their message heard. Douglas was teamed with M.J. Coldwell; they shared an office and were desk mates in

The CCF promised a better life for Canadians.

TOWARDS THE DAWN!

the Commons. They were also asked by leader J.S. Woodsworth to take responsibility for agricultural issues. It did not appear to matter that neither had ever run a farm. They seemed to qualify for the task for the simple reason that both were from Saskatchewan.

Douglas made his first speech in the House on 11 February 1936. During his remarks, he accused the new government of ignoring people on relief — how they had asked for bread and been given a stone. He also raised the topic of public health and talked about how people went without proper care because they did not have the money to pay for medical services. These problems would get only worse in Saskatchewan in 1937. A widespread drought resulted in an almost complete crop failure.

M.J. Coldwell and the CCF talked about the need for government planning.

As a member of a small caucus, Douglas was a frequent speaker who thrived in the give-and-take atmosphere on the floor of the Commons. One of his favourite targets was Jimmy Gardiner. The former Liberal premier of Saskatchewan had been recruited to serve as federal minister of agriculture in the new King government. He was also, like Douglas, famously short. One day, during a steady barrage of Liberal heckling led by Gardiner, the Weyburn MP retorted, "I don't want any more interruptions. If the Minister of Agriculture will sit up in his chair and dangle his feet, I'll go on with what I have to say." Gardiner never forgave him.

Douglas had gone to Ottawa to make things happen. He quickly chafed at the lack of parliamentary action on a number of issues and had little patience with Prime Minister King's plodding style of governing. "In those days of crisis," he complained, "it was most irritating to see his vacillation and failure to give any leadership." On the other hand, he developed a grudging admiration for former prime minister R.B. Bennett, a gifted orator who at least seemed interested in finding solutions.

Although Douglas was the agricultural critic for his party, he also waded into debates about Canadian foreign policy. The Italian dictator Mussolini had just invaded Ethiopia, and the Canadian delegate to the League of Nations (forerunner of the United Nations) had proposed the implementation of oil sanctions. The King government, however, refused to back the resolution, eliciting a stern response from Douglas who maintained that sanctions could be an effective deterrent to further aggression. This determination to meet fascist regimes head on would become more strident over the next few years and put the Weyburn MP at odds with his leader, J.S. Woodsworth, who was a declared pacifist.

In the summer of 1936, Douglas was sent to Geneva as one of three government chaperones for the Canadian contingent at the World Youth Congress. He used his three-month European visit to travel to Spain, where a civil war had just broken out. He also went to Nuremberg and watched in horror as German dictator Adolf Hitler presided over a parade of tanks and guns from the growing Nazi war machine. Douglas returned to Ottawa consumed by the sense of peril that Hitler posed to the world. "One cannot talk about conciliation with a mad dog," he warned. In a series of lectures about his trip, he called on Canada to end its isolationist stance in favour of some form of collective security.

By the late 1930s, war seemed imminent. Germany annexed Austria and then moved into Czechoslovakia. Great Britain, in the meantime, tried to avoid a confrontation, believing that Germany would be satisfied with the territory it had gained. Douglas was upset with Canadian support of British policy and about the danger of "yielding to dictators." One year later, when Germany invaded Poland on 1 September 1939, Great Britain and France declared war. Prime Minister King, in the interests of keeping the country united, had promised that, if war came, Canada would decide whether to participate. That time finally arrived the first week of September when Parliament was recalled to vote in a special emergency session.

The decision of whether Canada should go to war put the CCF in an extremely awkward position. Not only were Woodsworth and several other party members committed pacifists, but the Regina Manifesto declared that the party would not support any future imperialist wars. At the same time, it had become painfully clear that Hitler wanted to dominate Europe and that somehow the Nazi dictator had to be stopped.

Just before the parliamentary vote, the CCF held a two-day meeting in Ottawa to debate the matter of Canada's involvement. Woodsworth maintained his opposition to the war — any war — and declared his intention to resign as national leader if the party voted for participation. Many other members, however, were prepared to endorse a compromise position, which called on the Canadian government to offer political and economic support for the Allied war effort. Douglas was among them. "We've made certain gains, and if we say we will not use force to defend them, we could have them all taken away from us," Douglas maintained. "I recognized then that if it came to a choice between losing freedom of speech, religion, association, thought, and all things that made life worth living, and resorting to force, you'd use force."

A meeting of the CCF caucus in Ottawa. Douglas is seated at the far left.

Never Let Them Down

On 10 September 1939, Canada formally declared war against Nazi Germany. Woodsworth, who had been convinced to stay on as CCF leader despite his position, was the only member to speak against the government resolution in the House of Commons. Douglas joined the South Saskatchewan Regiment and was able to train in Weyburn and be close to his family. He was rejected for active service, though, because of his past knee problems and served as a reserve officer. The medical classification may have saved his life, since others from his battalion were sent to defend Hong Kong and died there when the Japanese invaded.

Douglas was re-elected with a larger majority in the March 1940 general election. In the months that followed, as the European situation worsened and France was overrun, CCF members increasingly supported the war effort, including sending troops overseas. They did not, however, support the suppression of Canadian civil liberties, especially when the government gave itself sweeping, secretive powers under the War Measures Act. Sadly, this concern did not extend to Japanese Canadians. In February 1942, following the Japanese bombing of Pearl Harbor and the entry of the United States into the war, the King government ordered the evacuation of all people of Japanese ancestry, including Canadian citizens, from a Pacific coastal zone and the confiscation of their property. Not one word of protest was heard from the CCF benches. Even Douglas was strangely silent.

Chapter 8
Is My Father the Premier Yet?

Apart from the absences from his family, Tommy Douglas enjoyed his years in Ottawa and the chance to debate federal and international issues. But because he was one of just a handful of CCF representatives, he made little impact on what one parliamentary journalist sarcastically called "the rhinoceros skin of government." Saskatchewan, on the other hand, seemed to offer greater opportunity, especially since the province was finally emerging from the shadow of the Depression. Indeed, it was the perfect challenge for someone like Douglas. Here was a place where the implementation of socialism by democratic means (known as democratic socialism) might be possible under the right circumstances.

Irma and young Shirley Douglas in their Weyburn home

The Weyburn MP had always kept one eye on the fortunes of the provincial Farmer-Labour Party (known as the Saskatchewan CCF since 1935). It was no temporary, flash-in-the-pan phenomenon as T.C. Davis had confidently predicted. Instead, the party moved to broaden its appeal by abandoning its contentious "use lease" land policy and placing greater emphasis on a planned

economy. This change was not without controversy. Some die-
hard supporters, disillusioned with the new direction, claimed
that the party had lost its sense of purpose.

The modified CCF platform did not prevent the Liberals
from returning to office in the 1938 provincial election. But the
ten seats won by the CCF confirmed that it was the only other
legitimate contender for power in the province. It needed better
organization, though, especially at the local level. It also needed
more funds if it was to fight a truly province-wide campaign.

Douglas, with the support of his Saskatchewan CCF friends,
was nominated as president of the provincial party at the 1941
convention. The opening had become available when the former

*Douglas (centre)
standing in front
of a CCF cam-
paign poster*

head of the party enlist-
ed and went overseas.
Douglas was elected
leader the following
year, while continuing
to hold down his seat in
Ottawa. He was not the
unanimous choice of the
party, especially among
hard-line socialists and
idealistic pacifists. He
would face critics from
both within and outside
the party. But his nine-
year apprenticeship in
Ottawa — he resigned

his seat in 1944 — had prepared him well for the rough-and-
tumble world of Saskatchewan politics.

Douglas did not expect to work miracles. "I thought it might
be possible to give the movement a shot in the arm," he reflected,
"and see it through the next election." But he had an immediate
impact on the CCF's chances by the sheer force of his personality.
It is doubtful that the party would have enjoyed the same degree
of success without the charismatic Douglas at the helm. He and
his team placed a premium on organization from provincial head-

quarters right down to local polling districts. New committees were established. Party memberships were sold. And a dedicated group of volunteer workers was recruited.

What ironically helped this organizing flurry was the provincial Liberal government's decision in 1943 to extend the life of the Legislature an extra year because of the war. The delay in calling the election gave the CCF more time to prepare, all the while righteously claiming that the Liberals were desperately clinging to office. In fact, it increasingly appeared that the government was bereft of ideas and interested only in preserving the status quo.

Douglas maintained that the Saskatchewan electorate needed a clear, consistent understanding of what to expect from a CCF government. This vision was particularly important as an Allied victory in the war seemed likely in 1944. People were worried that the coming of peace would bring with it another recession, as had been the case at the end of the Great War. They looked to government to provide stability, security, and prosperity in a post-Depression, post-war world. In other words, they wanted to build on the sacrifices and successes of the war years to capture the promise of the future and realize a better life.

The CCF was ready with a broad reform plan for postwar Saskatchewan. Since the last election in 1938, the party had further distanced itself from its radical beginnings. It now favoured a moderate program more in keeping with the needs and interests of Saskatchewan residents. But what made these policies particularly attractive was their comprehensiveness — they were like puzzle pieces, fitted together, into a coherent picture.

Tommy Douglas led the CCF to power in Saskatchewan in 1944.

In its campaign literature, the CCF did not talk simply about saving the family farm, but emphasized the need to put rural life on a sounder footing. It also spoke of using the state to bring about reform in education, health, and social welfare services. And it advocated diversifying the Saskatchewan economy, by state direction and management if necessary, to end the province's over-reliance on agriculture and thereby avoid another devastating depression.

The party's greatest asset in the years and months leading up to the election, however, was Tommy Douglas, who exuded confidence and forthrightness. He campaigned tirelessly to communicate the CCF message in town halls, on the streets, and at kitchen tables. "He had a smile," recalled a college friend, "and a way of dealing with people." He was equally sharp-witted and always had a quip, no matter what the occasion. At a Fir Mountain meeting, when his chair collapsed, spilling him on the platform, he dragged himself up, and rubbing his butt, announced, "Mr. Chairman, that is just where Mr. Gardiner's Liberals give me a pain."

Douglas also had a serious side, some would argue a stubborn sense of purpose. He had definite objectives and expected those around him to work just as hard as he did and to be just as committed. What kept him going was a sureness rooted in his faith and an unfailing conviction that a better world was possible. "The essence of Douglas lay in his idealism and in his capacity to inspire others with his sense of mission," a senior Saskatchewan civil servant remembered.

The Saskatchewan electorate finally went to the polls on 15 June 1944, just nine days after the Normandy invasion and the beginning of the end of the war. It was a beautiful, late spring day. The Liberals, poorly organized and lacking any inspirational policies, launched a vicious attack on the CCF, deliberately playing on public fears of communism and fascism. The Regina *Leader-Post* even warned that a socialist victory "may start Canada on the road to strife and devastation." Such tactics only sullied the Liberal image, especially when the CCF leader was a Baptist preacher, and CCF candidates and their supporters now represented a broad cross-section of the population. Besides, people wanted meaningful change, not defensive posturing.

Tommy Douglas

Shirley Douglas and her father

Douglas, who had invested so much time and energy in the campaign, viewed the election as fundamental to Saskatchewan's future. "This is the greatest political battle you and I have ever witnessed," he boldly announced in a radio address just days before the vote, "because the outcome may decide our way of life for the next quarter of a century."

Douglas spent election day at home with his wife and daughter. The returns from the heavy voter turnout were immediately telephoned to Weyburn by party workers across the province. Shirley Douglas kept bouncing into her dad's constituency office once the polls closed, innocently asking each time, "Is my father the premier yet?" She would not be disappointed. By ten p.m., the thirty-nine-year-old Douglas had stormed to office with a landslide victory. The CCF won forty-seven of fifty-two seats and fifty-three percent of the popular vote. Less than a month later, Douglas was sworn into office by another former premier, Saskatchewan Chief Justice William Martin.

Chapter 9
Making History

The CCF was elated about the decisiveness of its victory. "Saskatchewan is now all set to make history," boasted the *Saskatchewan Commonwealth*, the party's weekly newspaper. "The people in the province ... are ready for a new kind of government." What Saskatchewan got was an energized government led by a popular premier with an ambitious legislative program. It was as if Tommy Douglas and the CCF wanted to make up for the ground lost during the Depression and the war. In its first sixteen months in office, the new government approved a whopping 192 bills. A former civil servant reported that the machinery of government "groaned with overwork."

Premier Douglas chats with Canadian troops in England during the Second World War.

Much of what the Douglas government did during its first few years in office grew out of the campaign promise to bring about a planned economy. To achieve this goal, Saskatchewan underwent a kind of revolution in how government administration operated. The CCF was the first government of a Canadian province to introduce the idea of integrated government planning and budgeting. It also developed a professional public service. In fact, many of the new civil servants in the Douglas government had come from across North America, attracted to the province by the opportunity to be a part of the bold Saskatchewan experiment. Among them was future premier Allan Blakeney.

In an effort to lessen the province's dependence on agriculture, the new CCF government went on a shopping spree. It purchased a Regina shoe factory and tannery, Moose Jaw woollen mill, and Prince Albert box factory — even a defunct brick plant in Estevan. These government-owned enterprises were supposed to help bring about a more diversified economy for the benefit of all citizens. But the new manufacturing ventures could not compete against cheaper out-of-province imports, and it was not long before they began to lose money and went out of business. As Douglas admitted years later, "We did too much ... trying to bring about social ownership in almost every aspect of human life, instead of tackling two or three fields."

The CCF government had a more enviable record in other areas. It established a compulsory automobile insurance plan (Saskatchewan Government Insurance), one of several firsts in Canada. It also incorporated rural and municipal telephone companies into Saskatchewan Government Telephones. And it launched a provincial bus company. All have become part of the provincial fabric and continue to operate to this day.

The Douglas family on holiday at their cottage

The Douglas government did not neglect cultural matters. In 1945, it passed the Saskatchewan Archives Act, which created an agency to collect and preserve material about the province's past. It also approved the Western Development Museum Act, which provided funding for four branch museums in the province. Today, the collection features over 65,000 artifacts, mostly from the province's settlement period; many are part of Saskatoon's "Boom Town" exhibit, a replica 1910 streetscape. The CCF government's most heralded initiative, however, was the 1948 creation of the Saskatchewan Arts Board, the first agency of its kind in North America. Modelled after the British Arts Council, the Arts Board was designed to provide provincial residents with more opportunity to participate in creative activities like art, literature, and drama.

Douglas's reform agenda did not escape criticism. The Liberal Opposition ominously warned that "outside" planners had assumed control of the government. It also fervently took up the banner of "free enterprise." This strategy attempted to divide Saskatchewan politics along strict ideological lines by appealing to Cold War fears and the threat posed by Soviet Russia at the time. For the Liberals, CCF socialism was just one step away from communism, Regina just one edict away from becoming another Moscow. This socialism versus capitalism debate would dominate provincial politics for decades.

Douglas was able to fend off these attacks in part because he learned from his missteps. From its first days, the CCF had recognized that it had to adjust and be flexible if it was going to achieve office and maintain its electoral appeal. That's exactly what the premier did in office. The failure of the shoe business and other fiascoes made him wary of investing any more public funds in potentially risky projects. It made more sense to concentrate on public ownership of utilities and other services and leave more competitive development to private enterprise — what is known as a mixed economy.

Douglas also had the good fortune of being in office when non-renewable resources were being developed in the province. Revenue from oil and natural gas, along with increased mineral production, especially uranium, filled the provincial treasury in the 1950s. The new resource developments helped diversify the provincial economy. They also helped Saskatchewan recover more quickly from the debt load it carried from the Great Depression.

The most important thing that the CCF had going for it in Saskatchewan was Tommy Douglas. In many respects, he was both the government and the party — or at least it seemed that way because of the heavy workload he carried. He spent as much as twelve hours a day at the Legislature, usually walking from his home six blocks away. He often returned to his office in the evenings after supper and a short nap. Saturdays were devoted to government business in the morning and party matters in the afternoon. On Sunday nights, he visited the sick in hospital. He often ended up there himself for a few days each year because of exhaustion, made worse by recurring problems with his knee.

Douglas also continued to give speeches at every opportunity. He regularly embarked on official speaking tours when not pressed into service by local party organizations. He was always ready with a joke or a story, such as the political allegory called "Mouseland," to inspire the CCF faithful. His best performances, though, were usually reserved for his opponents, particularly during election campaigns. When Walter Tucker, the Saskatchewan Liberal leader, made a disparaging comment about the premier's height, a smiling Douglas retorted, "Mr. Tucker is big enough to swallow me, but if he did he would be the strangest man in the world. He would have more brains in his stomach than he does in his head."

Despite his busy schedule, the premier remained an extremely accessible leader, whose door was always open to the people of

Tommy Douglas's office at the Saskatchewan Legislature. Douglas kept a photo of American president Abraham Lincoln on the fireplace mantle.

Saskatchewan and who insisted on personally answering the many letters he received. There was also nothing fancy about Douglas. If he was working in the Legislature, he invariably took his lunch in the basement cafeteria and always had the same standing order: poached eggs, tomato juice, and prunes. Official visitors sometimes joined him in line and dined on trays at the arborite tables. Behind the friendly exterior, though, was a leader who expected results and had no time for excuses.

Douglas's efforts were rewarded at the polls. Beginning in 1944, he won five consecutive mandates (1944, 1948, 1952, 1956, 1960), something that has never been achieved since in Saskatchewan political history. These election victories seemed to validate the course that he had charted for the province since the mid-1940s. More importantly, they were a testament to the premier's popularity. Douglas appeared destined to lead his party and govern the province for as long as he wanted.

Premier Douglas escorts Queen Elizabeth during a royal visit to Regina in 1951.

Tommy Douglas

Chapter 10
Chief Red Eagle

In the 1944 Saskatchewan election, the CCF ran on the motto "Humanity First." It was no simple election slogan. The Douglas government reflected the spirit of the postwar period when western democracies sought to use their influence and intervention to bring about a better world. In the case of the Saskatchewan CCF, its goal was nothing less than to create the "conditions under which individual freedom and human well-being might flourish."

One of the major tests of the Douglas government was the province's First Nations population. "It has been said that the measure of any society is what it does for the least fortunate group," the premier once observed. "It is not enough ... to raise the standard of living if there continues to remain ... a small, underprivileged, diseased, illiterate minority in society." Doing something, though, would not be easy or straightforward since First Nations were the responsibility of the federal government. It would also mean reversing decades of federal coercion and control.

A young First Nations boy from Saskatchewan

Since the late nineteenth century, the Canadian government had effectively prevented First Nations from participating in the larger Saskatchewan society. They could not leave their reserves without first securing a pass. Nor could they market any of their produce without first securing a permit. Federal officials also believed that there was little in First Nations culture that was worth saving. Children were to be assimilated at residential schools, while traditional religious practices were banned. First

Nations regarded these federal policies as a blatant violation of the treaty agreements they had signed with the Crown in the 1870s.

By the 1930s, Saskatchewan's First Nations people had not disappeared as a distinct group as predicted, but were actually growing in number. They were frustrated, however, not only with their marginal status, but also with the pervasive federal interference in their lives. John Tootoosis of the Poundmaker Reserve worked tirelessly to organize First Nations throughout the decade. He also spearheaded a campaign demanding that the government address treaty grievances made worse by the Great Depression. But these efforts only earned him a hostile reception from Ottawa and a reputation for being a troublemaker.

The province's First Nations people looked to Douglas for help shortly after he assumed office. They not only named the new premier an honorary chief, Red Eagle, but indicated that they were interested in working through his office to establish a new, province-wide organization that would give them a voice in running their own affairs. Douglas readily agreed and used his influence to convene a meeting of Saskatchewan First Nations delegates. The Regina conference, held in the legislature cafeteria, endorsed the idea of a single provincial body. But it took another two meetings, the second one in Saskatoon in 1946 and

Premier Douglas was made an honorary chief, Red Eagle.

Tommy Douglas

the largest gathering of chiefs and councillors in provincial history, before the Union of Saskatchewan Indians (USI) was formally established.

Douglas hoped that bringing the province's First Nations together in a new organization would serve as a springboard for meaningful change in their lives. After all, First Nations soldiers had fought overseas during the war to defeat Nazism only to return home to discrimina-tion in Canada. But the fed-eral government continued to administer them with a heavy hand. The new Saskatchewan organization learned this sorry truth first-hand. Agents from the Department of Indian Affairs throughout the province were meeting with Ottawa officials in Saskatoon the day after the founding USI con-vention. When John

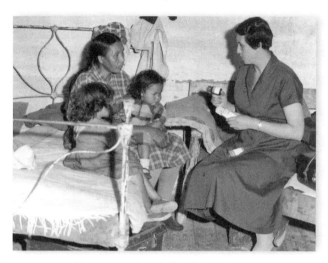

A nurse visits a First Nations family.

Tootoosis, fresh from his election as president, asked to join the discussions, he and several chiefs were shooed away with the warning that there would be "no talking with Indians."

The Douglas government was becoming increasingly un-happy, if not uneasy, with the situation of the province's First Nations. In 1947, the Saskatchewan Legislature had approved a Bill of Rights — the first in Canada — that prohibited discrimi-nation on racial and religious grounds. But any euphoria associat-ed with the landmark bill was dampened by the reality of the First Nations people, who were segregated and living in poverty, with few prospects of work and facing a hopeless future.

Douglas was appalled by conditions on Saskatchewan's reserves and looked for a way of ensuring that First Nations received the same level of services enjoyed by other provincial citizens. He could not accept the fact that one segment of Saskatchewan's population was living apart from the rest of provincial society. It was just not the CCF way. "We don't settle all the Chinese people out in ... some corner of the province," he noted in reference to the reserve system.

The CCF government established the Committee on Indian Affairs in 1956. It immediately produced a report that called for, among other things, the transfer of responsibility for First Nations to provincial jurisdiction. At the heart of this initiative, according to Douglas, was the principle that they "integrate into white society." He wanted First Nations to be full and equal partners in Saskatchewan society.

It was a noble objective. But what the premier failed to do, like other well-meaning politicians both in the past and in the future, was to consult with the First Nations themselves. And what worried John Tootoosis and many other First Nations leaders was that integration might adversely affect their status. In other words, they were prepared to participate in the larger provincial society, but not if it came at the expense of their treaty rights, traditions, and culture.

Premier Douglas addressing a meeting of Saskatchewan's First Nations leaders

For the remainder of his term as premier, Douglas pursued integration as the answer to discrimination against First Nations. He also continued to help them organize — as a step towards their eventual absorption into mainstream society. John Tootoosis welcomed this government assistance. But he used the help to promote a new, independent provincial body, the Federation of Saskatchewan Indians, which made treaty rights its foremost concern. It was an ironic outcome to Douglas's efforts.

Chapter 11
Down on the Farm

Another major challenge for the Tommy Douglas government was securing the future of rural Saskatchewan. The widespread adoption of farm machinery after the Second World War and the movement to larger holdings had encouraged people to leave the countryside in record numbers. Agriculture was beset with instability, but the most troubling development was the shuffling of rural society to the margins of postwar Canada. Saskatchewan, the most rural of Canada's western provinces, had to find its way in a new world where rural life was seen as backward, lacking in opportunity, but worst of all, in decline. As comedian Groucho Marx mockingly asked, "How're you gonna keep 'em down on the farm ... after they've seen the farm?"

Joking aside, the statement had an element of truth to it. When measured against the new standards of the 1950s, Saskatchewan was out of step with the urban, modern, affluent Canada of the postwar world. The province — the so-called Last Best West — had once been considered Canada's future, but those days were past. "Saskatchewan," wrote Nipawin-born writer Sharon Butala, "was only a holding area where one waited impatiently till one

Premier Douglas wanted to bring rural Saskatchewan into the modern age.

was old enough to leave in order to enter the excitement of the real world."

From the perspective of the CCF government, the solution was quite simple: provide rural folks with the same level of services and quality of life as their urban counterparts, which would reduce, if not slow down, migration from the region. It was a tall order, but one that Douglas did not shrink from.

The Douglas government started in the field of education. When Saskatchewan's population peaked in the mid-1930s, there were about 5,000 school districts in the province. Most were rural, one-room schools, where the teacher juggled eight grades, while sometimes supervising older students who were taking high school courses by correspondence. During the Depression, the buildings were allowed to deteriorate. Then the war took away hundreds of qualified teachers who volunteered for duty.

The CCF wanted to reverse this situation by bringing about a higher level of education and providing better access to education. It also had to get kids back in schools. Dozens of rural schools were closing because they lacked teachers, were run-down, or farms were being abandoned.

The obvious answer, as far as Douglas and his colleagues were concerned, was to move to "larger school units." But parents complained that the loss of local schools would be another blow

Premier Douglas opening a new bridge across the South Saskatchewan River

Tommy Douglas

to their rural communities. The government refused to reconsider its policy. At the start of the 1950s, one in five one-room schools was being closed annually; by the end of the decade, the rate was two out of every five.

Another initiative to improve rural services and provide a degree of stability was the rebuilding of the province's road system. Saskatchewan had over 160,000 kilometres of roads — more per capita than the other three western provinces combined. But the roads had badly deteriorated during the Depression and desperately needed upgrading; by the start of the 1950s, the province had less than 1,600 kilometres of paved highway. The government set itself the goal of constructing a province-wide system of all-weather grid roads, and by 1964 had chalked up more than 20,000 kilometres.

In the meantime, Saskatchewan Government Telephones expanded and upgraded the provincial system through the 1950s and started work on a microwave system to be tied into the national network. These efforts may not have dispelled rural isolation, but farm families could at least take comfort from the thought that help was just a phone call away. Television, on the other hand, was an urban novelty. The first stations began broadcasting in the province in 1954, but reception was largely restricted to the immediate Regina, Moose Jaw, and Saskatoon areas.

Under the Family Farm Improvement Program, the Douglas government also provided financial assistance to farm families and towns and villages to install sewage and water systems. These kinds of improvements were long overdue. At the start of the 1950s, only one in five farm homes had running water, let alone a bathroom. The situation in smaller communities was just as bad.

Much of rural Saskatchewan did not have electricity at the end of the Second World War.

56

The CCF's most ambitious revitalization program, as set out in the Rural Electrification Act of 1949, was to provide electricity to 50,000 farms and all towns and villages by 1960. Many observers scoffed at the idea because of the immensity of the task, especially when potential customers were so sparsely settled. The Saskatchewan Power Corporation, however, tackled the rural electrification program with military-like organization. While crews fanned out over the province, the corporation tried to promote the use of electricity by mailing out information on how electricity could improve agriculture and enhance home life. It also distributed a booklet on home wiring.

The arrival of a SaskPower construction crew in a district was a much anticipated event. Rural residents often invited crew members to take part in baseball games, curling, or some local event. And romances sometimes developed. One construction foreman reported three weddings between crew members and local women one year. Workers were also honoured guests at "lights on" parties.

There was resistance, though. Some rural residents had never seen electrical appliances, while many more were afraid of electricity. To ease these concerns, the company created a home services division and hired Lillian McConnell, more popularly known as Penny Powers. Through a slick promotional campaign, Penny

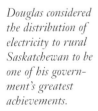

Douglas considered the distribution of electricity to rural Saskatchewan to be one of his government's greatest achievements.

Tommy Douglas

Powers extolled the benefits of electricity in columns and letters, and toured the province giving practical demonstrations of the uses of electricity.

Penny's efforts won over rural women and power lines were run to farm houses. It was no coincidence that ninety percent of the electricity initially consumed in rural districts was for domestic purposes. The first purchases were usually a refrigerator, ending decades of trying to keep food fresh in an ice box, or an electric pump to bring running water from the well indoors. To encourage the purchase of dryers, SaskPower adopted the slogan, "Clothes lines are for the birds."

By 1956, all towns and villages in southern Saskatchewan were served with power. Two years later, Saskatchewan Power Corporation reached its target of 50,000 farms. Electricity literally energized local businesses — from signs to store windows to inside lighting. Children no longer complained about dimly lit rural schools, while sporting and cultural activities in rural areas were no longer restricted by the lack of light. Some people, however, remained uneasy about electricity. One girl, left at home alone for the first time, remembered her parents turning off the power at the pole before they headed to town. Another farm family had only one light bulb and would move it from room to room wherever a light was needed.

Tommy Douglas rightly regarded the electrification of rural Saskatchewan as one of his greatest achievements. But in the end, despite all that had been done to improve the quality of life in rural Saskatchewan, his government could not stop the out-migration. The rate of rural population loss in the 1950s might not have been as great as during the 1940s, but people were still leaving the farm, especially adolescents. High school, radio, movies, and even all-weather roads introduced young people to another world beyond the farm and what they were missing. Many could not wait to get away.

Chapter 12
The Road to Medicare

When Tommy Douglas took office in Saskatchewan in 1944, he also took on the health portfolio. This double duty underscored the importance of health care to the new CCF government. "We believe ... we can ultimately give our people a completely socialized system of health services," Douglas had pledged in a radio address the year before the provincial election, "irrespective of ... individual ability to pay." As Saskatchewan premier, he was determined to ensure that no one ended up in the same predicament he had faced as a young boy when he nearly lost his leg to osteomyelitis because of a lack of money. Equal access to quality health care was intended to prevent such tragedies.

Premier Douglas speaking at a hospital opening in the 1950s

By the time of the CCF victory, Saskatchewan already had the distinction of pioneering a number of health care firsts. Beginning in 1916, the provincial government allowed rural municipalities to hire doctors and pay them a fixed fee to retain their services for the local community. That same year, it enabled towns, villages, and rural municipalities to come together to establish and maintain "union hospitals." Over time, while traditional fee-for-service medicine held sway in Saskatchewan cities, a form of socialized medicine took root and flourished in the countryside; rural districts set and collected health taxes, built and managed hospitals, and hired and paid medical personnel.

Premier Douglas, as health minister in his own government, wanted to take medical care in the province to another level and immediately commissioned a health services survey. The new government used the report to fashion a number of health initiatives in the first few years of its mandate: free cancer treatment (1944); comprehensive health care for people on social assistance, including pensioners and spouses (1945); and an air ambulance service (1946). The crowning achievement, the introduction of Canada's first universal hospital insurance program in 1947, offered a complete range of hospital benefits to Saskatchewan's residents for an annual premium.

Douglas relinquished the health portfolio in 1949. But the cost of providing a full medical care insurance plan was still too prohibitive at the time, especially with the province struggling to get back on its economic feet after the Depression and war. That all changed in the late 1950s, thanks to buoyant resource revenues and increased federal transfers, and a federal commitment to pay half

A rally against medicare at the Saskatchewan Legislature

the cost of the existing hospital insurance plan. The premier now jumped at the opportunity to introduce medicare. "If we can do this — and I feel sure we can," he told a provincial radio audience in December 1959, "Saskatchewan [will] lead the way. Let us therefore have the vision and the courage to take this step ... toward a more just and humane society."

The CCF medical care insurance program was to be based on five principles: prepayment of costs, universal coverage, high quality service, public administration, and a form of service acceptable to both providers and recipients. On this last point, Douglas believed that the government and the province's doctors could reach an amicable agreement. But the medical community declared that it was adamantly opposed to any compulsory scheme that threatened to put the profession under government control.

In an effort to blunt the doctors' opposition, Douglas called an election on the issue in June 1960. When the CCF was easily returned to office for a fifth term, the premier interpreted the victory as a mandate to introduce medicare. But there was no consensus on how best to proceed. The introduction of the legislation was also complicated by the departure of Tommy Douglas from provincial politics.

The national CCF was about to join with organized labour to form the New Democratic Party, and the premier was being courted to lead the new federal party. But Douglas was reluctant to abandon his Saskatchewan career until medicare was in place. "I have started a big job here," he said during a newspaper interview, "and I would like to finish it if people will let me." That seemed unlikely. Just days before Douglas officially took over the NDP helm, the CCF government finally introduced the Saskatchewan Medical Care Insurance bill. The doctors warned that trouble lay ahead and vowed not to co-operate. The premier, however, was not prepared to back down and advised his successor, Woodrow Lloyd, to proceed with the legislation.

Douglas resigned in early November 1961 to take up his new post after a remarkable seventeen years as premier. His departure was deeply regretted by many in Saskatchewan, not only for all that he had done for the province, but because his political skills and personal integrity would likely be needed to defuse the explosive medicare issue. But Lloyd was a worthy successor and tried to bring the medical association on side, but without success.

On 1 July 1962, the day the legislation came into effect, doctors suspended their services, except for limited emergency care at some hospitals. In their place stepped British physicians who had been recruited by the Lloyd government.

In the first days of the strike, there was considerable public unease, fed by the uncertainty of what was going to happen. Some citizens had formed "Keep Our Doctors" committees in June and talked of forcing the CCF government to withdraw the medicare act. Premier Lloyd resolved to ride out the medicare storm, believing that the doctors' demands could not override the larger interests of Saskatchewan society.

FRANKENSTEIN

A political cartoon published during the medicare crisis

Finally, three weeks into the strike, a British doctor assumed the role of mediator and spent several days bringing the politicians and doctors together and finding common ground. By July 23, the two warring parties had signed the Saskatoon Agreement, which preserved the principle of universality, while removing those sections of the legislation that implied government control of doctors. The CCF government immediately reconvened the Legislature, and in one of the shortest sessions in Saskatchewan history, it amended the medicare act in accordance with the agreement.

Tommy Douglas's dream had been realized. So too would his prediction that medicare would be adopted nation-wide when the

Douglas and Woodrow Lloyd, his successor as premier of Saskatchewan

federal government approved the Medical Care Act in 1966.
But even though he had done so much to bring medicare about
— to the point where his name is so closely identified with it
today — he was not in the premier's chair when Saskatchewan
implemented the scheme.

Chapter 13
Finest Hour

Tommy Douglas got off to a rocky start as the first leader of the New Democratic Party. Although he was the overwhelming choice of the delegates at the party's founding convention, he suffered a humiliating defeat in Regina in the federal election in June 1962. Many political commentators attributed his loss to the bitterness over the introduction of medicare. Douglas was stoic about his fate at the hands of the electorate. "I'll lay me down and bleed awhile," he said, quoting an old Scottish ballad during his concession speech on television, "and then I'll rise and fight again."

Douglas entered the House of Commons later that fall after winning a by-election in British Columbia. He would serve in Parliament for seventeen years, the first ten as leader of the

Douglas speaking at the founding NDP convention

NDP. When his past service as Weyburn MP is included, he spent twenty-six years in federal politics — much longer than his term as premier. In fact, following his 1962 defeat, he never tried to run again in Saskatchewan despite his long association with the province. What also tends to get overlooked was that his return to Ottawa represented quite a change in his life. Here was a man who had ruled Saskatchewan as if it was his own fiefdom starting over at the bottom again.

From the beginning, Douglas tried to carry the new party on his back. It was tough slogging. As one of his former speech writers confessed years later, "The NDP's only real political weapon" was the leader's "wit, eloquence, and passion." Douglas began all his rallies with a few anecdotes, some of which the crowd could recite from memory. What the public did not understand, though, was that the seeming spontaneity of the stories was the product of careful preparation. Or that he continued to be

Douglas, as federal NDP leader, on the campaign trail in the early 1960s

dogged by the after-effects of his childhood osteomyelitis, especially during cold, damp weather. His weekends were usually spent resting in seclusion with his wife, Irma.

Despite his herculean efforts, Douglas made little headway as leader of the new party. Although Canadians were unable to decide between the Liberals and Conservatives and endured a series of minority governments in the 1960s, the former Saskatchewan premier was unable to take advantage of the situation. Like its CCF predecessor, the NDP seemed destined to be the country's perennial third party. In time, Douglas's leadership came to be questioned, especially when the Liberals under Pierre Elliott Trudeau secured a massive victory in 1968. In comparison, the folksy, bespectacled Douglas seemed a geezer, a holdover from a distant yesterday. Not even his infectious smile could compete with Trudeau's rebel image.

Douglas tried to be a voice of reason and compassion in the House. In 1965, he called for the American withdrawal from the Vietnam War and the opening of peace negotiations. This stance made him the darling of the Canadian left and a featured speaker at Canadian anti-war rallies. But it also gave encouragement to a splinter group within the federal party, known as the Waffle movement, which called for an independent, socialist Canada. The infighting between more moderate members of the party and the younger, more radical Waffle would hurt the NDP.

Douglas's "finest hour," according to a documentary film maker, came during the 1970 October Crisis. Early that month, terrorists belonging to the Front de Libération du Québec (FLQ), bent on revolutionary change in the province, kidnapped the British trade commissioner in Montreal. Several days later, they struck again, kidnapping the Quebec minister of labour. The Trudeau government responded on 16 October by proclaiming the War Measures Act and sending troops into Quebec. More than 450 people were rounded up and detained; most were never charged.

The War Measures Act had been invoked only twice before — when Canada was at war in 1914 and 1939. Now the legislation was being used to deal with a domestic emergency by a prime minister reputed to be a civil libertarian. Most members of the House of Commons, including representatives from Quebec, applauded the move. Douglas, however, was steadfastly opposed, especially when he believed that Ottawa had mishandled the situation. To repeated shouts of "Shame, shame" from MPs in the House, he tried to explain that the government had other ways to deal the crisis. "We are not prepared to use the preservation of law and order as a smokescreen to destroy the liberties and freedom of the people of Canada," he argued. "The government, I submit, is using a sledgehammer to crack a peanut."

Douglas's comments were greeted with outright hostility. He was accused of being disloyal in the face of a national emergency, of trying to win votes at a time when the government was vulnerable. In general, most Canadians believed that they had nothing to fear from the government's hard-nosed response. But with the passage of time, many came to appreciate Douglas's position during those troubled weeks. "It was Tommy Douglas of the NDP," recalled Eric Kierans, a former federal and Quebec Liberal politician, "who stood in the House, day after day, and hammered the government for suspending civil liberties, and if you ask me today why I wasn't up there beside him, I can only say, 'Damned if I know.' He showed political courage of the highest order."

Douglas stepped aside as leader of the party in 1971. It seemed that, at sixty-seven, his work was done. It was time to retire, spend more time with his family, including grandchild Kiefer Sutherland, the son of daughter Shirley and actor Donald Sutherland. But Douglas, the old boxer, still had a few more rounds to go before he stepped out of the ring. Indeed, the NDP found itself holding the balance of power in 1972 when a somewhat humbled Trudeau was returned to office at the head of a minority government.

Douglas was one of Canada's greatest orators.

Tommy Douglas

Only Stanley Knowles (far right) served longer than Douglas as a CCF/NDP Member of Parliament in the House of Commons.

The chance for the NDP to flex its newfound muscle in Parliament came during the so-called energy crisis. In 1973, the new Organization of Petroleum Exporting Countries (OPEC) imposed a partial oil embargo and jacked up world oil prices. Douglas, who served as energy critic for his party, suggested that the country should move to self-sufficiency in oil and use the vehicle of a government-owned oil company as a way of getting there. The Trudeau government not only gave in to the demand, but presented the idea of a national petroleum company as a Liberal solution to the country's energy woes. When Petro-Canada was eventually created in July 1975, Prime Minister Trudeau called Douglas and the NDP "a bunch of squawking seagulls" for trying to take credit.

Douglas continued to preach the virtues of energy self-sufficiency through the 1970s, even after public enthusiasm for the idea had waned. He also spoke out against the Trudeau government's multimillion dollar scheme to build a natural gas pipeline down the Mackenzie Valley because of its impact on northern society. He lost more battles than he won, but had the respect of the House as an elder statesman. Douglas announced in 1976 that he would not be seeking re-election. Three years later at the age of seventy-five, he closed the door on his parliamentary career.

Tommy Douglas was not really meant for retirement, but like everything else, he worked at it. He and Irma began to spend more time at their cottage in the nearby Gatineau Hills, and treated themselves to annual winter holidays in Florida.

In the summer of 1981, Douglas was diagnosed with inoperable cancer. He took the news in stride and refused to slow down. It was not his style. At the NDP convention in Regina in 1983, he was the guest of honour at the party's commemoration of the adoption of the CCF's Regina Manifesto fifty years earlier. He delivered what became known at "the speech."

It was an old-style political sermon. Reflecting on the tough times that the party had faced, Douglas warned about the current threat to medicare and then told the 2,000 members not to lose faith. "We are seeking to get people who are willing to dedicate themselves to build a different kind of society," Douglas thundered, "a society founded on the principles of concern for human well-being and human welfare."

In early February 1986, Douglas put on his suit and went by car to Parliament Hill for the last time. He never ventured outside again and was dead before month's end.

Tributes poured in from across the country. NDP leader Ed Broadbent broke the news to the House of Commons the same day Douglas died. "He never despaired, no matter what the obstacle," said Broadbent on 24 February. "That exuberant and hopeful spirit, based on the deep conviction that society should be organized for the benefit of all people ... is what took him through all the obstacles in his long and remarkable life."

But it was Tommy who provided the most telling assessment of his life. When asked in 1970 about the failure of the NDP to

Tommy Douglas was voted the Greatest Canadian in a CBC television poll in 2004.

achieve power in Ottawa, he said: "Sometimes people say to me, 'Do you feel your life has been wasted?'... And I look back and think that a boy from a poor home on the wrong side of the tracks in Winnipeg was given the privilege of being part of a movement that changed Canada. In my lifetime I have seen it change Canada."

Maybe that's why Tommy Douglas was selected as the Greatest Canadian — over John A. Macdonald, Alexander Graham Bell, Wayne Gretzky, and other prominent individuals — in a CBC television poll in 2004. Surely, so many Canadians could not be wrong.

Tommy Douglas – Timeline

1904: Born on 20 October in Falkirk, Scotland

1911: Emigrates to Winnipeg

1914: Spends Great War in Scotland

1919: Witnesses Winnipeg General Strike and Bloody Saturday riot

1924: Enters Brandon College to train as Baptist minister

1930: Becomes preacher in Weyburn, Sask., and marries Irma Dempsey

1933: Attends first convention of new CCF party

1934: Birth of daughter Shirley

1935: Elected to House of Commons as CCF MP for Weyburn

1944: Leads CCF to victory in Saskatchewan provincial election

1947: Passage of Saskatchewan Bill of Rights

1948: Creation of Saskatchewan Arts Board

1949: Rural Electrification Act approved

1959: Announces plan to establish Medicare

1961: Resigns as premier of Saskatchewan to lead federal NDP

1962: Medicare introduced by Lloyd government in Saskatchewan

1970: Speaks out against War Measures Act during October Crisis

1971: Steps down as federal NDP leader

1979: Retires from Parliament

1986: Dies of cancer on 24 February

2004: Voted Greatest Canadian in CBC television poll

Tommy Douglas, 1940s

Further Reading

Evelyn Eager, *Saskatchewan Government: Politics and Pragmatism*
(Saskatoon: Western Producer Prairie Books, 1980).

A.W. Johnson, *Dream No Little Dreams: A Biography of the Douglas Government
in Saskatchewan, 1944-61* (Toronto: University of Toronto Press, 2004).

Thomas McLeod and Ian McLeod, *Tommy Douglas: The Road to Jerusalem*
(Edmonton: Hurtig Publishers, 1987).

Doris Shackleton, *Tommy Douglas* (Toronto: McClelland and Stewart, 1975).

Walter Stewart, *The Life and Political Times of Tommy Douglas*
(Toronto: McArthur, 2003).

Lewis H. Thomas, *The Making of a Socialist: The Recollections of T.C. Douglas*
(Edmonton: University of Alberta Press, 1984).

Robert Tyre, *Douglas in Saskatchewan: The Story of a Socialist Experiment*
(Vancouver: Mitchell Press, 1962).

Bill Waiser, *Saskatchewan: A New History* (Calgary: Fifth House Publishers, 2005).

Acknowledgments / Photo Credits

The author would like to thank David Fairbairn, Allan Blakeney, Bill Brennan,
Jim Miller, Ali Roberts, and David Smith for reading and commenting on an
early draft of the book. The author also wishes to recognize Linda Biesenthal for
her careful work in shepherding the manuscript through the production stages.

Hugh McPhail, 55; Library and Archives Canada, pages 22, 23, 30, 37, 49, 63,
67; Manitoba Archives, pages 6, 7, 8, 10, 11, 12; Saskatchewan Archives Board,
pages 4, 17, 21, 24, 25, 26, 27, 29, 33, 34, 39, 40, 41, 43, 44, 45, 47, 48, 50, 51,
52, 53, 54, 58, 59, 62; *Saskatoon Star-Phoenix*, 61; University of Saskatchewan
Archives, 35, 56; Western Canada Pictorial Index, pages 16, 64, 66, 69.

Index